X

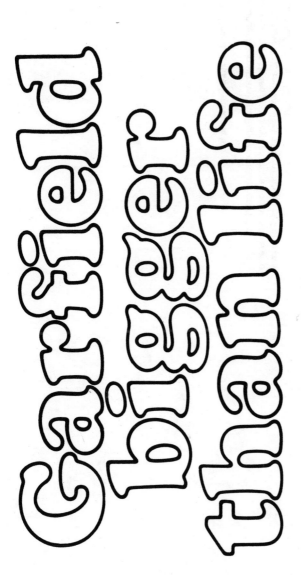

Garfield bigger than life

BY: JIM DAVIS

BALLANTINE BOOKS · NEW YORK

Library of Congress Catalog Card Number: 81-066659

ISBN 0-345-32007-7

Manufactured in the United States of America

First Ballantine Books Edition: November 1981

40 39 38 37 36 35 34

SAY, YOU LOOK LIKE YOU WANT TO GO JOGGING THIS MORNING, GARFIELD

YOU ARE WRONG, SWEAT SOCK BREATH

8-27

JOGGING IS FINE FOR SOME PEOPLE, I SUPPOSE...

© 1979 United Feature Syndicate, Inc.

BUT I'VE NEVER BEEN THAT CRAZY ABOUT THE DRY HEAVES

© 1979 United Feature Syndicate, Inc. JIM DAVIS

KERCHUNK!

8-28

A NEW WORLD'S RECORD

© 1979 United Feature Syndicate, Inc.

WHEN WAS THE LAST TIME YOU STUCK 44 KEYS ON A TYPEWRITER?

JIM DAVIS

GARFIELD ATE MY TOOTHPASTE AGAIN

OH, GREAT

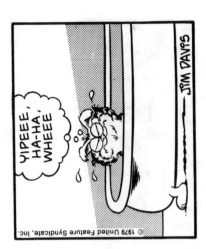

JIM DAVIS

8-29

© 1979 United Feature Syndicate, Inc.

I JUST LOVE TO COURT DANGER

8-30

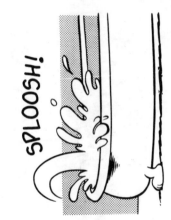

SPLOOSH!

YIPEEE, HA-HA, WHEEE

JIM DAVIS

© 1979 United Feature Syndicate, Inc.

THIS IS MY PET ANT, LYLE. HE'S CUTE, QUIET, AND INDUSTRIOUS

8-31

JIM DAVIS

WHAT?! WHERE?!

SPLAT!

HE DID IT AGAIN

JIM DAVIS

THE "LATE" LYLE WAS ALSO EYEBALLING MY LASAGNA

9-1

NOT **THE BOX**!!!

JIM DAVIS

SCUFFLE
SCUFFLE
STRUGGLE
GRAB!
STUFF
STUFF

OH, ♪ GARFIELD

© 1979 United Feature Syndicate, Inc.

WE'RE GOING ON A TRIP, GARFIELD, SO JUST HOP INTO YOUR NEW KITTY CARRIER HERE

LET ME PUT IT TO YOU THIS WAY. BEFORE WE GO ON THE TRIP ONE OF US IS GOING TO HAVE TO GET INTO THIS KITTY CARRIER

WELL WHY DIDN'T YOU SAY SO?

9-2

GUESS WHAT, GARFIELD? WHILE MOM AND DAD'RE ON A WEEK'S VACATION, WE'RE GOING TO BABY-SIT FOR THEIR KITTEN

MEET NERMAL

© 1979 United Feature Syndicate, Inc. JPM DAV9S

WAKE ME IN A WEEK

I GOTTA SPEND A WEEK WET-NURSING NERMAL, HERE... HE'S CUTE

© 1979 United Feature Syndicate, Inc.

AND I HATE "CUTE"

JPM DAV9S

DON'T KNOCK IT, JACK. I MAKE A KILLING POSING FOR GREETING CARDS

9-4

9-3

OH, NERMAL.
NERMAL.
NERMAL.

OKAY, NERMAL.
THERE'S A DOG.
...KILL!

© 1979 United Feature Syndicate, Inc.

9-5

I CAN'T STAND
CAT HAIRS UNLESS
THEY'RE MY OWN

NERMAL SHED
ALL OVER
MY FOOD

CRUD!

© 1979 United Feature Syndicate, Inc.

9-6

NERMAL'S LEAVING NOW. WAVE BYE-BYE, GARFIELD.

9-8

TAKE THOSE ROLLER SKATES OFF, GARFIELD. YOU LOOK RIDICULOUS.

9-7

I KIND OF LIKED THE LITTLE FELLER

THE WAY I LIKE INTESTINAL FLU

JIM DAVIS

SOME PEOPLE SAY PETS ARE NOT CLEAN

© 1979 United Feature Syndicate, Inc.

9-15

THAT MAY BE SO

JIM DAVIS

ODIE, YOU KNOW BETTER THAN THAT

© 1979 United Feature Syndicate, Inc.

9-14

DO YOU KNOW WHAT I APPRECIATE ABOUT YOU MOST, GARFIELD?

I'M HOUSEBROKEN

YOU'RE HOUSEBROKEN

JIM DAVIS

BUT TRY EATING YOUR NEXT MEAL WITHOUT YOUR HANDS AND SEE HOW WELL YOU FARE

OUT OF THE CLOSET, YOU FATTIES!

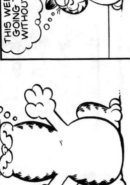
THIS WEEK WE'RE GOING TO EAT WITHOUT GUILT

© 1979 United Feature Syndicate, Inc.
9-25

I AM HEREBY DECLARING THIS COMING WEEK "NATIONAL FAT WEEK"

CARTOONIST'S NOTE:
TODAY'S GARFIELD STRIP IS TO BE READ ONLY BY FAT PEOPLE, OR PEOPLE WITH FAT TENDENCIES. YOU SKINNY ONES CAN READ THE OTHER STRIPS, OR JOG, OR DRINK A GLASS OF WATER, OR WHATEVER IT IS SKINNY PEOPLE DO.
...I WOULDN'T KNOW.

I WOULD HAVE HAD A NATIONAL CONVENTION

BUT I COULDN'T GET THE KANSAS CITY STOCKYARDS TO CATER IT

JIM DAVIS

WE'LL BOYCOTT CARROTS AND TELL SKINNY JOKES

REMEMBER OUR SLOGAN: "IF IT'S NOT DEEP-FRIED, IT'S NOT WORTH EATING."

BE CAREFUL THERE, GARFIELD

© 1979 United Feature Syndicate, Inc.

HANGING ON THE DRAPES CAN BE VERY PAINFUL

'CAUSE I'M GONNA BREAK YOUR LEGS IF YOU DON'T GET OFF THEM THIS INSTANT!

9-24

GASP! CHOKE! WHEEZE!

9-25

OH NO YOU DON'T, GARFIELD

SO MUCH FOR THE OLD "PLAY-SICK-AND-GRAB-THE-CHICKEN-WHEN-YOUR-OWNER-CALLS-THE-VET" ROUTINE

JIM DAVIS

© 1979 United Feature Syndicate, Inc.

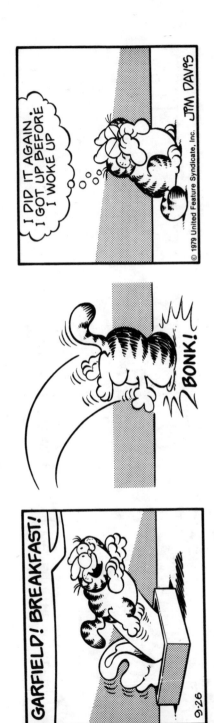

GARFIELD! BREAKFAST!

9-26

© 1979 United Feature Syndicate, Inc.

I DID IT AGAIN.
I GOT UP BEFORE
I WOKE UP

© 1979 United Feature Syndicate, Inc.

BONK!

STOMP!

WAG
WAG
WAG

9-27

JIM DAVIS

WAG
WAG
WAG

9-28

MEYOWWW

LET ME GUESS. YOU WERE IN THE PICKLED HERRING AGAIN

JIM DAVES

9-29

EAT UP, GARFIELD

MEYOW

GARFIELD

IT SAYS HERE THIS IS A "NEW IMPROVED" CAT FOOD

MUNCH MUNCH

GARFIELD

MEYOW!

GARFIELD

JIM DAVES

WE'RE GOING TO SEE YOUR VETERINARIAN TODAY, GARFIELD

10-1

THAT LIZ IS SURE A GREAT LOOKING HUNK OF VETERINARIAN

SHE'S ONE CUTE CHICKY-BOO. I'D MARRY HER IN A SECOND

SHE HAS THE ONE QUALITY I DESIRE MOST IN A WOMAN

SHE'S BREATHING

10-2

JIM DAVIS

IT'S COMFORTING TO KNOW THE HIGH VALUES PLACED ON THE SACRED INSTITUTION OF MARRIAGE ARE STILL WITH US TODAY

IN A HALF-SECOND!

JIM DAVIS

BE RIGHT WITH YOU, MR. ARBUCKLE

© 1979 United Feature Syndicate, Inc.

I'LL BE HERE WITH BELLS ON, DOCTOR

THAT MAKES FOR AN INTERESTING MENTAL PICTURE

WHY DOES SHE ALWAYS PUT ME DOWN?

YOU'RE SO PUTDOWNABLE

JIM DAVIS

10-3

HOW ABOUT GOING OUT WITH ME, DOCTOR?

I WOULDN'T GO OUT WITH YOU IF YOU WERE THE LAST MAN ON EARTH

10-4

THEN HOW ABOUT SOMETIME AFTER THAT?

THAT'S A GOOD ONE

JIM DAVIS

© 1979 United Feature Syndicate, Inc.

WHY WON'T YOU GO OUT WITH ME, DOCTOR?

BECAUSE I HATE YOUR GUTS

JIM DAVIS © 1979 United Feature Syndicate, Inc.

10-5

DOES THIS MEAN MARRIAGE IS OUT OF THE QUESTION?

DON QUIXOTE STRIKES AGAIN

HOW ABOUT A DATE, DOC?

NO WAY

10-6

(MMMMM)

JIM DAVIS © 1979 United Feature Syndicate, Inc.

GREAT! SEE YOU AT EIGHT

IF YOU CAN'T CONVINCE 'M, CONFUSE 'M

I SUPPOSE YOU WANT TO KNOW HOW MY DATE WENT WITH LIZ. THE VET...WELL, DON'T ASK

I WON'T

10-8

MUNCH MUNCH MUNCH

10-9

SHE DIDN'T SHOW. OLD JON GOT STOOD UP

I DON'T WANT TO HEAR ABOUT IT

© 1979 United Feature Syndicate, Inc.   JIM DAViS

SMACK! SLURP! GOBBLE!

YOU KNOW, GARFIELD, I LIKE YOU BETTER THAN PEOPLE

TELL ME MORE

© 1979 United Feature Syndicate, Inc.   JIM DAViS

MY AUNT EVELYN IS THE NEATEST CAT I KNOW

SHE PLUCKED ALL THE HAIR OFF HER BODY SO SHE WOULDN'T SHED ON THE FURNITURE

NOW SHE'S LIVING WITH A FAMILY IN L.A. THAT THINKS SHE'S A CHIHUAHUA

JIM DAVIS

10-10

YIP! YIP! YIP!

FOR THE LAST TIME, ODIE, YOU CHASE THE TAIL

JIM DAVIS

10-11

YIP! YIP! YIP!

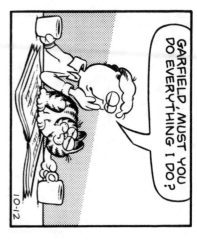

GARFIELD, MUST YOU DO EVERYTHING I DO?

10-12

10-13

© 1979 United Feature Syndicate, Inc.

THAT WASN'T VERY NICE

FWIP FWIP FWIP FWIP FWIP

SHOOP!

AFTER ALL, CATS ARE JUST LITTLE PEOPLE WITH FUR AND FANGS

JIM DAVIS © 1979 United Feature Syndicate, Inc.

A VENETIAN TONGUE

JIM DAVIS

WAKE UP, SLEEPYHEAD!

WE'RE HAVING BREAKFAST ON THE PATIO THIS MORNING

BECAUSE I WANT TO SHARE THIS BEAUTIFUL SUNRISE WITH YOU

JIM DAVIS

10-14

HAVE YOU EVER SEEN A MORE GLORIOUS SIGHT, GARFIELD?...UH, GARFIELD?

WHERE ELSE CAN YOU FIND A LIVING, BREATHING WORK OF ART CREATED JUST FOR YOU? FRESH WITH THE PROMISE OF A BRIGHT NEW DAY

GET YOUR FACE OUT OF THE SCRAMBLED EGGS, GARFIELD

ZZZZ

© 1979 United Feature Syndicate, Inc.

BATH TIME, GARFIELD

10-15

GOTCHA!

10-16

SQUIP!

© 1979 United Feature Syndicate, Inc.

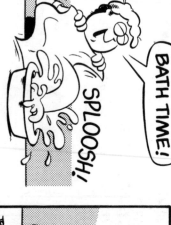

(BATH TIME!)

SPLOOSH!

LARD

JIM DAVIS

NOW WHERE COULD POOKY BE?

JIM DAVIS © 1979 United Feature Syndicate, Inc.

MORNIN'

GOOD MORNING, IRMA

10-19

THE COFFEE'S STRONG, HON. YOU'D BETTER GET IT BEFORE IT GETS YOU

IS IT HOT?

© 1979 United Feature Syndicate, Inc.

THIS ISN'T ONE OF YOUR BETTER DINERS

YUP

MY, YOU LOOK NICE TODAY, IRMA

ARE YOU KIDDING?

10-20

WHEN I COME TO WORK I WEAR BASE AND LIPSTICK AND THAT'S IT, HON. I DON'T PUT ON EYES UNLESS I HAVE A HOT DATE. YOU KNOW WHAT I MEAN?

© 1979 United Feature Syndicate, Inc.

I DIDN'T EVEN SHAVE MY LEGS

THIS DEFINITELY ISN'T ONE OF YOUR BETTER DINERS

JYM DAVYS

10-23

HEY, GARFIELD, WHERE'S ODIE?

HE'S EASY ENOUGH TO FIND

JUST FOLLOW THE SLOBBER

JIM DAVIS

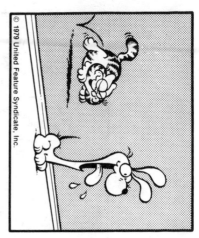

10-22

SMACK!

I HATE PATIO DOORS

JIM DAVIS

GOOD BOY, GARFIELD. GIVE ME THE PAPER

© 1979 United Feature Syndicate, Inc.

10-29

© 1979 United Feature Syndicate, Inc.

EITHER I GET BREAKFAST OR YOU'LL NEVER SEE THIS PAPER ALIVE AGAIN

FLIP!

I CAN TAKE A HINT

10-30

JIM DAVIS

WHY IS THERE ALWAYS A STRING ATTACHED?!

NOTHING'S FREE, PAL

JIM DAVIS

LET'S GO SEE THE VET, GARFIELD

I HAVE A TEN O'CLOCK APPOINTMENT

JIM DAVIS

11-2

HERE, PETEY. HERE, PETEY. WHERE ARE YOU?

VETERINARY CLINIC

BURP!

JIM DAVIS

11-3

PACK YOUR BAGS, GARFIELD. WE'RE GOING ON VACATION

© 1979 United Feature Syndicate, Inc.

11-5

I WISH YOU ENJOYED RIDING IN A CAR MORE

© 1979 United Feature Syndicate, Inc.

WE HAVE A LONG WAY TO GO, GARFIELD

JIM DAVIS

GOOD IDEA

YOU'RE TOO TENSE

11-6

I COULD USE THE REST

JIM DAVIS

JIM DAVIS

I'D LIKE A ROOM FOR THE NIGHT

ANY PETS?

NOPE

...UH, THINK

LOOK AT THAT, GARFIELD. WHAT DO YOU...

JIM DAVIS

WHEN I THINK OF SAND, I THINK OF SUN, SURF, AND GETTING A GOOD TAN

11-10

WHAT DO YOU THINK OF WHEN YOU THINK OF SAND, GARFIELD?

FRED'S FRESH FISH

11-9

ON SECOND THOUGHT, SCRATCH THAT QUESTION

JIM DAVIS

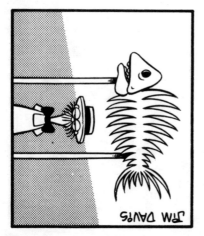

JIM DAVIS

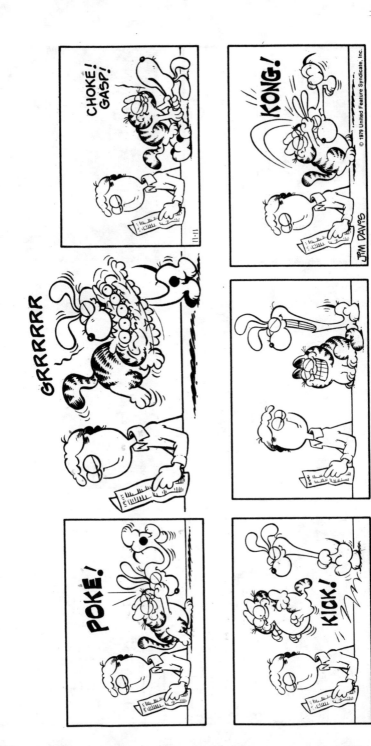

rain (rān) *n.* **1.** water falling to earth in drops

SCREECH!

2. a mild depressant

CHASING CARS AGAIN, GARFIELD?

11-13

11-14

11-15

I HATE IT WHEN GARFIELD FALLS ASLEEP IN MY LAP

ZZZ

11-17

HE SNUGGLES UP

ZZZ

AND DIGS IN

ZZZ

JIM DAVIS

© 1979 United Feature Syndicate, Inc.

HOW'S YOUR COFFEE, HON?

IT'S A BIT STRONG

SAY IT'S NOT SO! SAY IT'S NOT SO! I COULD JUST SHOOT MYSELF!

11-16

© 1979 United Feature Syndicate, Inc.

YOU USUALLY DON'T FIND ONE THAT DEDICATED

IT'S HER LIFE

JIM DAVIS

AH-AH-AH

JIM DAVIS

© 1979 United Feature Syndicate, Inc.

AHCHOO!

SNIFF

11-19

SCRATCH THE SOFA ALL YOU LIKE, GARFIELD

JIM DAVIS

REVERSE PSYCHOLOGY

© 1979 United Feature Syndicate, Inc.

REVERSE REVERSE PSYCHOLOGY

11-20

I OFTEN WONDER WHAT GOES ON IN THAT COMPLEX MIND OF YOURS, GARFIELD

BZZZZZZZZZZZZZZZZ

THAT'S A NASTY COLD YOU HAVE THERE, GARFIELD

SNIFF

© 1979 United Feature Syndicate, Inc.

JIM DAVIS

WOULDN'T IT BE WONDERFUL IF HUMANS AND ANIMALS COULD COMMUNICATE?

SMACK!

© 1979 United Feature Syndicate, Inc.

JIM DAVIS

WE'LL TAKE YOU TO THE VET AND GET YOU FIXED RIGHT UP

WHAT WOULD YOU SAY TO ME IF YOU COULD TALK RIGHT NOW?

I JUST KILLED A FLY SOMEWHERE ON YOUR RAISIN TOAST

11-23

NEVER SAY "FIXED" TO AN ANIMAL PERSON

11-24

GET OFF THE CEILING, GARFIELD

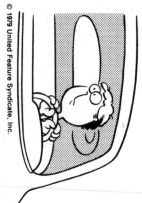

GET BACK IN THE GLOVE COMPARTMENT, GARFIELD

11-26

GET OUT OF THE GLOVE COMPARTMENT, GARFIELD

GET YOUR FACE OFF THE WINDSHIELD, GARFIELD

11-27

© 1979 United Feature Syndicate, Inc.

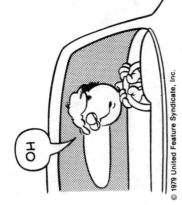

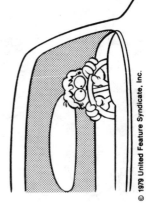

DINNER'S ON, GARFIELD. WE HAVE LASAGNA AND CHICKEN AND MASHED POTATOES

11-30

WELL, GARFIELD, THAT'S THE LAST TIME THE HAMILTONS EVER ASK US OVER

© 1979 United Feature Syndicate, Inc.

JIM DAVIS

LET'S SEE, I THINK I'LL HAVE...

© 1979 United Feature Syndicate, Inc.

I HOPE YOU LEARNED A LESSON FROM THIS EVENING

I SURE DID

A PEANUT BUTTER AND JELLY SANDWICH

NEVER SHARPEN YOUR CLAWS ON A WATER BED

12-1

GUESS WHO'S COME TO VISIT US THIS WEEK, GARFIELD?

12-3

NERMAL! THE WORLD'S CUTEST KITTEN

© 1979 United Feature Syndicate, Inc.

JIM DAVIS

HOW CUTE!

12-4

YOU'RE TESTING ME, AREN'T YOU?!

© 1979 United Feature Syndicate, Inc.

JIM DAVIS

HOW CUTE!

HOP HOP HOP

SOMEHOW GARFIELD, YOUR GRASP OF "CUTE" IS A LITTLE SHAKY

JIM DAVIS

12-5

BOOM! BOOM! BOOM!

THERE'S ONE NICE THING ABOUT HAVING ANOTHER CAT AROUND THE HOUSE

12-6

NERMAL!

SCRATCH! SCRATCH! SCRATCH! SCRATCH!

JIM DAVIS

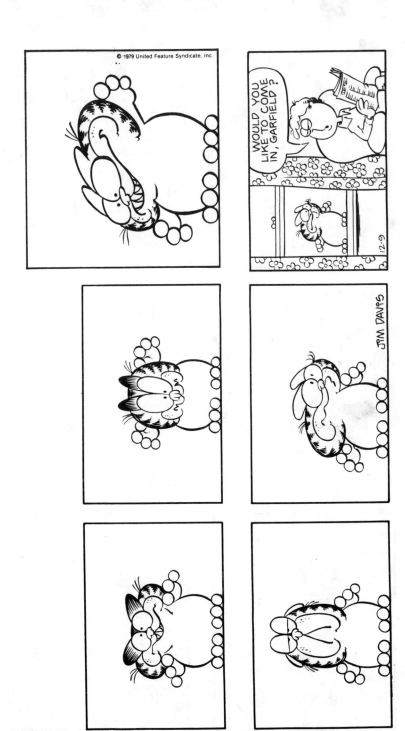

PLIP!

HOT! HOT! HOT!

JIM DAVIS

JIM DAVIS

12-11

IT'S TIME WE TALKED ABOUT THIS COFFEE DEPENDENCY OF YOURS, GARFIELD

AHHH

12-10

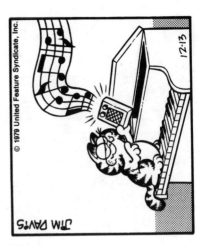

© 1979 United Feature Syndicate, Inc.

12-12

GET OFF THE PIANO, ODIE. YOU'RE MAKING TOO MUCH RACKET

© 1979 United Feature Syndicate, Inc.

12-13

WE'LL GO ON THE ROAD. WE'LL MAKE A MILLION! WE'RE RICH!

GARFIELD! THAT'S BEAUTIFUL!

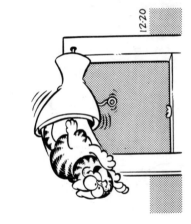

JUST ONE BITE OF CHICKEN
AND THAT'S IT, GARFIELD

12-24

© 1979 United Feature Syndicate, Inc.

WHATEVER YOUR BELIEFS,
THE CHRISTMAS SEASON
REPRESENTS PEACE, LOVE
AND CHARITY AMONG PEOPLE
EVERYWHERE

12-25

MERRY CHRISTMAS
AND SEASON'S GREETINGS

IF YOU SWALLOW,
I'LL TIE A KNOT
IN YOUR NECK

JIM DAViS

SOMETIMES I'M
SO SENTIMENTAL
I COULD JUST
KISS MYSELF

JIM DAViS © 1979 United Feature Syndicate, Inc.

THIS YEAR I RESOLVE
TO LOSE WEIGHT...

12-31

JIM DAVIS

TO BE NICER
TO DOGS...

AND TO
SPROUT WINGS
AND FLY

SO THIS
IS 1980

1-1

FEELS ABOUT
THE SAME

JIM DAVIS

© 1980 United Feature Syndicate, Inc.

JUST AS I SUSPECTED

1-4

THE FLOOR IS FREEZING

CLOP!

CLOP!

GARFIELD

© 1980 United Feature Syndicate, Inc.

JIM DAVIS

1-5

AHCHOO!

BACK OFF, GARFIELD. THAT TURKEY LEG IS FOR MY LUNCH

WOULD YOU LIKE A TURKEY LEG, GARFIELD?

ONLY IF YOU DON'T WANT IT

JIM DAVIS

SCRATCH SCRATCH SCRATCH SCRATCH SCRATCH SCRATCH

© 1980 United Feature Syndicate, Inc

1-6

WIPE WIPE WIPE WIPE

WHAT WOULD YOU LIKE FOR BREAKFAST, GARFIELD?

SOMETHING DIFFERENT!

© 1980 United Feature Syndicate, Inc.

1-8

THE USUAL, YOU SAY?

NO! NO! NO! NO!

ONE USUAL COMING UP!

IT'S THINGS LIKE THIS THAT CONTRIBUTE TO THE HIGH SUICIDE RATE AMONG CATS

JIM DAVIS

SLURP!

© 1980 United Feature Syndicate, Inc

THE COFFEE'S TOO HOT GARFIELD.

THANKS FOR TELLING ME

JIM DAVIS

1-7

HOW MANY TIMES HAVE I TOLD YOU NOT TO BEG AT THE TABLE?

OH, NO, GARFIELD. YOU'RE NOT GETTING MY CHICKEN TODAY

I KNOW ALL YOUR PLOYS, BUDDY BOY. I'M WATCHING YOU LIKE A HAWK

SOMETIMES OPIE IS A REAL PROBLEM

JIM DAVIS

JIM DAVIS

I WISH I HAD YOUR PROBLEM

SNIFF

OH DOE! I'M CUBBING DOWN WID A CODE

LOOG, I CAN HARDLY EBBEN UNDERSTAD BY OWN THOUGHTS

JIM DAVIS

SNIFF

OH, ICKY POO! GARFIELD'S GOT A COLD HE'S DISEASED! EVERYONE STAND BACK!

BERRY FUDDY

JIM DAVIS

YOUR COUGH
SOUNDS BETTER,
GARFIELD

HACK
HACK

IT SHOULD

1-19

JIM DAVIS

I'VE BEEN
PRACTICING
ALL NIGHT

SNIFF

1-18

ARRRGH!!!

COLDS CAN BE
FRUSTRATING,
CAN'T THEY,
OL' BUDDY?

JIM DAVIS

EAT MY MASHED POTATOES!

MY CHICKEN!!!

AS LONG AS YOU ATE MY CHICKEN, GARFIELD, WHY DON'T YOU...

AND MY RADISHES! AND MY CELERY!

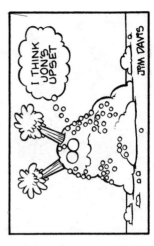

I THINK JON'S UPSET

AND MY PEAS!

JIM DAVIS

1-20

GARCON, I'LL HAVE THE ESCARGOT AND TRUFFLES FOR AN APPETIZER, THEN THE DUCK À L'ORANGE FLAMBÉ AND SOME CAPPUCCINO

JIM DAVIS © 1980 United Feature Syndicate, Inc.

CRASH!

1-26

HERE'S YOUR COFFEE, HON

EAT UP, PAL

GARFIELD

© 1980 United Feature Syndicate, Inc. JIM DAVIS

THIS ROLLER SKATING CRAZE IS GETTING OUT OF HAND

TALK ABOUT LOWERING ONE'S SIGHTS...

GARFIELD

1-25

READY FOR TENNIS?

AS SOON AS I FEED GARFIELD. HE'S HUNGRY.

HERE'S A PICTURE OF GARFIELD AT THE ZOO

HOW DO YOU KNOW THAT?

HERE'S GARFIELD SITTING NEXT TO A VERY RARE #300 PARROT

I HAVE MY WAYS

HERE'S A PICTURE OF ME SHELLING OUT 300 BUCKS FOR GARFIELD'S LUNCH

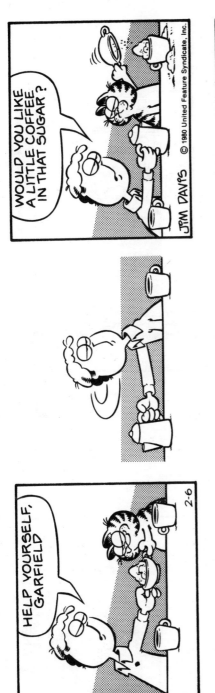

WOULD YOU LIKE A LITTLE COFFEE IN THAT SUGAR?

HELP YOURSELF, GARFIELD

HEH HEH, HOW NICE

THIS SHOULD BLOW JON'S MIND. ME, GARFIELD, BEING NICE TO ODIE

PAT PAT

THAT WAS A JOKE, YOU TWIT

PAT PAT

JIM DAVIS © 1980 United Feature Syndicate, Inc.

2-6

2-7

© 1980 United Feature Syndicate, Inc.

OOPS, I CRUNCHED JON'S ANTENNA

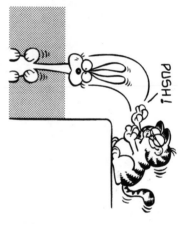

PUSH!

A LITTLE MORE TO THE RIGHT, GARFIELD

© 1980 United Feature Syndicate, Inc.

JIM DAVIS 2-9

POOMP!

2-8

THIS TABLE WASN'T BIG ENOUGH FOR THE BOTH OF US

JIM DAVIS

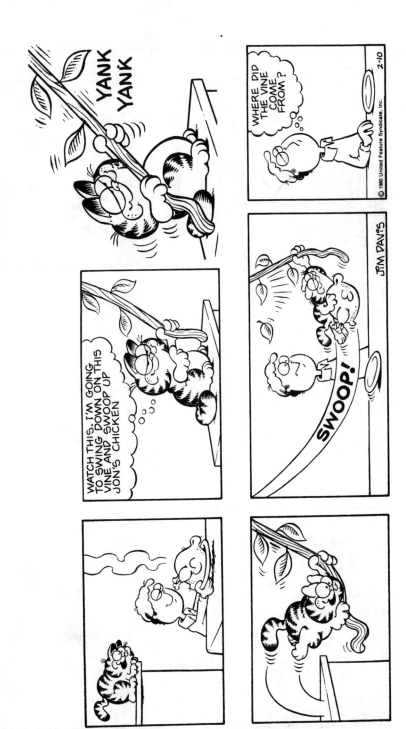

GUESS WHAT, GARFIELD? THIS WEEK WE'RE GOING TO VISIT DAD AND MOM ON THE FARM

© 1980 United Feature Syndicate, Inc.

2-11

YIPEE SKIP

THERE'S ONLY ONE THING YOU HAVE TO REMEMBER WHEN WE GET TO THE FARM, GARFIELD

WATCH WHERE YOU STEP

2-12

LET ME OUT

I THINK I'LL CALL IN SICK THIS WEEK

© 1980 United Feature Syndicate, Inc. JIM DAVIS

JIM DAVIS

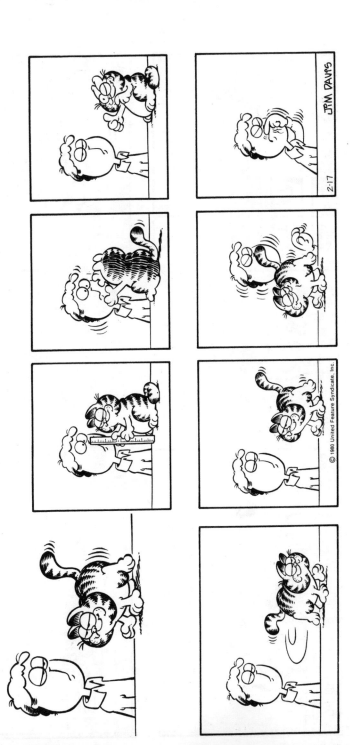

THIS WOULD BE A GOOD MORNING FOR A BRISK WALK

JIM DAVIS

2-18

TO THE FOOD DISH

© 1980 United Feature Syndicate, Inc.

CLACK!

LIFE WASN'T HALF AS MUCH FUN BEFORE I GOT MY YO-YO BONE

JIM DAVIS

© 1980 United Feature Syndicate, Inc.

2-19

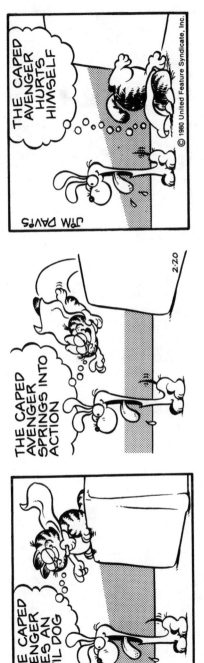

WE'RE HAVING LASAGNA FOR DINNER TONIGHT, GARFIELD

JIM DAVIS

© 1980 United Feature Syndicate, Inc.

PTOOEY!

WHAT SAY I BAKE IT FIRST

WHAT SAY

2-22

THIS IS GREAT. YOU'D MAKE SOMEONE A GOOD WIFE

I COULD USE A GOOD BACK WALK, GARFIELD

2-25

JIM DAVIS

© 1980 United Feature Syndicate, Inc.

NO CLAWS! NO CLAWS!

2-25

YOU'RE TOO FAT, GARFIELD. I'M PUTTING YOU ON ANOTHER DIET

HE MAKES ME SO MAD

IF I COULD HAVE GOTTEN UP ON THAT CHAIR, I WOULD HAVE GIVEN HIM THE BEATING OF HIS LIFE

JIM DAVIS

© 1980 United Feature Syndicate, Inc.

2-26

HERE'S A CARROT FOR YOUR DIET, GARFIELD. YOU KNOW WHAT TO DO WITH IT

I CERTAINLY DO

JIM DAVIS

HERE RABBIT, RABBIT, RABBIT

© 1980 United Feature Syndicate, Inc.

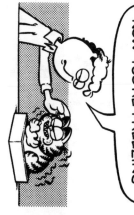

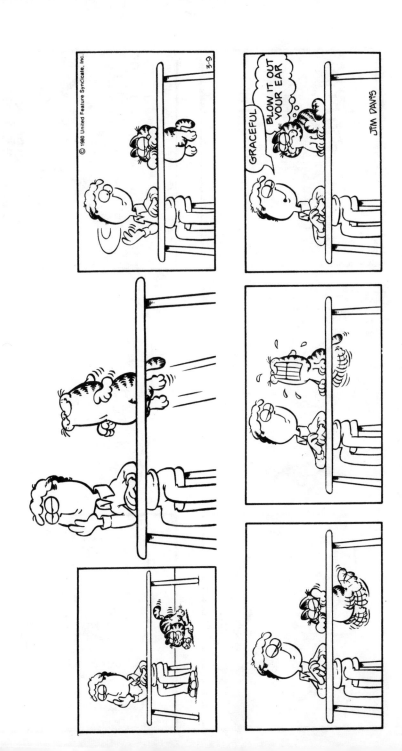

THIS LOOKS LIKE IT'S GOING TO BE A GOOD WEEK

JIM DAVIS © 1980 United Feature Syndicate, Inc.

3-10

NUTS... NUTS, NUTS, NUTS

© 1980 United Feature Syndicate, Inc.

MEYOW

3-11

LISTEN TO THAT

PURRR

JIM DAVIS

THE KID'S A WALKING CLICHE

FFFT

AWW, HOW CUTE

RIP RIP RIP

WHIP!

JM DAVS

3-12

LET ME REPHRASE THAT

DRIBBLE DRIBBLE DRIBBLE

3-13

GARFIELD, YOU SHOULD LEARN TO PLAY WITH NERMAL

SURE THING

HOP HOP

JM DAVS

HERE, NERMAL.
DO SOMETHING.
MORE CONSTRUCTIVE
WITH YOUR TIME

JIM DAVIS

© 1980 United Feature Syndicate, Inc.

3-14

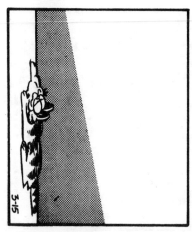

SAY GOOD-BYE TO
GARFIELD, NERMAL

~ SMACK ~

JIM DAVIS

© 1980 United Feature Syndicate, Inc.

3-15

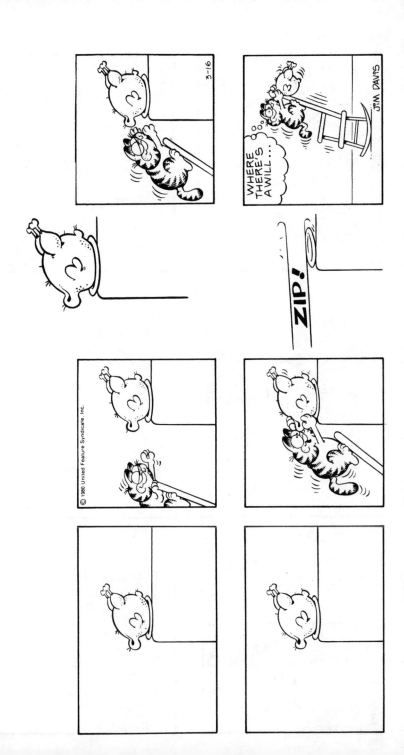

GARFIELD, GET YOUR LAZY BONES OUT OF BED AND COME TO BREAKFAST

SCRAPE
SCRAPE
SCRAPE

SCRAPE
SCRAPE
SCRAPE

3-17

IS THAT ALL I AM TO YOU?

MERELY AN OBSTRUCTION IN THE ROAD OF LIFE

3-18

I KNOW YOU CATS ARE INQUISITIVE BY NATURE, GARFIELD

AND I KNOW THIS IS YOUR HOME AS WELL AS MINE...

BUT STAY OUT OF MY UNDERWEAR DRAWER!!

3-19

JIM DAVIS

COMPUTERS... EVERYTHING IS CONTROLLED BY COMPUTERS THESE DAYS

THAT CHICKEN YOU ATE WAS EVEN RAISED BY A COMPUTER

burp

3-20

JIM DAVIS

THEY'LL PROBABLY WANT YOU TO DO TRICKS AT THE CAT SHOW, GARFIELD. SO HOP THROUGH THIS HOOP

I COULD JUST CRY

JTM DAVTS   © 1980 United Feature Syndicate, Inc.

HURRY UP, GARFIELD! TIME TO LEAVE FOR THE CAT SHOW

GRRR   ROWR

© 1980 United Feature Syndicate, Inc.   3-29

YIP! ROWR! FFT!

3-28

I COULD JUST CRY

JTM DAVTS

Garfield Up Close and Personal

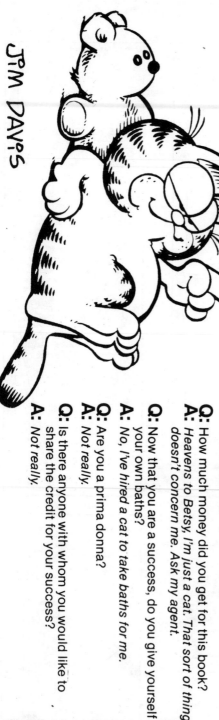

JiM DAViS

Q: What is your favorite sport?
A: *Each morning, before breakfast, I like to take a good, brisk nap.*

Q: Where did you get your nasty temper, and why are you so cynical?
A: *Step a little closer and ask that.*

Q: Describe your relationship with Jon, Odie, Pooky, and Nermal.
A: *Someone to abuse, someone to pound on, someone to confide in, and no comment.*

Q: Why did you call your most recent book "GARFIELD Bigger Than Life"?
A: *I didn't name the book, actually. I have the distinct feeling it is some kind of slur on my size. The book was named by my late editor.*

Q: How much money did you get for this book?
A: *Heavens to Betsy, I'm just a cat. That sort of thing doesn't concern me. Ask my agent.*

Q: Now that you are a success, do you give yourself your own baths?
A: *No, I've hired a cat to take baths for me.*

Q: Are you a prima donna?
A: *Not really.*

Q: Is there anyone with whom you would like to share the credit for your success?
A: *Not really.*